This

book

belongs

to :

_____

Unless otherwise indicated, all Scripture quotations are taken from The ESV® Bible (The Holy Bible, English Standard Version®), copyright © 2001 by Crossway, a publishing ministry of Good News Publishers. Used by permission. All rights reserved.

Verses marked NIV are taken from the Holy Bible, New International Version®, NIV®. Copyright © 1973, 1978, 1984, 2011 by Biblica, Inc.® Used by permission. All rights reserved worldwide.

Cover by Nicole Dougherty

Interior design by Janelle Coury

Published in association with William K. Jensen Literary Agency, 119 Bampton Court, Eugene, Oregon 97404.

GraceLaced Seasons

Copyright © 2018 Artwork and Text © by Ruth Chou Simons
Published by Harvest House Publishers
Eugene, Oregon 97408
www.harvesthousepublishers.com

ISBN 978-0-7369-7490-5 (pbk.)

Printed in China

18 19 20 21 22 23 24 25 26 / RDS-JC / 10 9 8 7 6 5 4 3 2 1

Name three aspects of God's character
that allowed you to rest in His presence and
not fear in that season.

On God rests my salvation and my glory;
my mighty rock, my refuge is God.
Trust in him at all times, O people;
pour out your heart before him;
God is a refuge for us. *Selah*

PSALM 62:7-8

These verses tell us why we find security and rest in
God and what to do in response to those truths.

What is said about our God in verse 7?

_____

_____

_____

_____

What does David, the writer of this psalm,
say to do in response (verse 8)?

_____

_____

_____

_____

_____

_____

_____

"Pour out your heart before him" here,
knowing God is your refuge:

_____

_____

_____

_____

_____

_____

_____

_____

_____

_____

_____

_____

_____

_____

_____

_____

_____

_____

Those who know your name put their trust in you,
for you, O LORD, have not forsaken those who seek you.

PSALM 9:10

If we are to trust in God, we must know who He is—
which His names reveal. The Bible tells us that He is our
Father, our Redeemer, our Counselor, our Friend.

Which of the names of God above (or others
from the Bible) do you need to rest in right now,
so that you might trust Him more?

Many are the sorrows of the wicked,
but steadfast love surrounds the one who trusts in the LORD.

PSALM 32:10

We lean on the Lord and not on ourselves, and are therefore
upheld by all that is of His character and not our own. Begin
a list here (and keep adding to it!) declaring the steadfast love
God has and continues to surround and uphold you with.

I was with you in weakness and in fear and much trembling, and my speech and my message were not in plausible words of wisdom, but in demonstration of the Spirit and of power, so that your faith might not rest in the wisdom of men but in the power of God.

1 CORINTHIANS 2:3-5

In what way do you feel insufficient today?

Paul says his insufficiency is a "demonstration of the Spirit." Describe one way that the insufficiency you feel has led you to rely on the power of God.

Pen a prayer asking the Lord to demonstrate His power through your weakness, that people around you might be convinced of His faithfulness—not as a result of your own wisdom, but of God's power.

Be strong in the Lord and in the strength of his might. Put on the whole armor of God, that you may be able to stand against the schemes of the devil. For we do not wrestle against flesh and blood, but against the rulers, against the authorities, against the cosmic powers over this present darkness, against the spiritual forces of evil in the heavenly places.

EPHESIANS 6:10-12

Let's not allow lies to ensnare us or weaken our faith, friends.
When we feel lacking or weak,
we must turn to Christ for our defense.

Write down one area of battle in your life where your strength feels inadequate for the task.

_____

_____

Apply the armor of God to this battle and jot down ways you can put on each of these provisions of defense:

Belt of truth

_____

_____

_____

Breastplate of righteousness

_____

_____

_____

Gospel of peace as footwear

Shield of faith

Helmet of salvation

Sword of the Spirit

Prayer—praying at all times

I know how to be brought low, and I know how to abound. In any and every circumstance, I have learned the secret of facing plenty and hunger, abundance and need. I can do all things through him who strengthens me.

PHILIPPIANS 4:12-13

What are the "all things" you are learning to do in His strength?

What skills or resources do you lack? What
should you do when facing need?

When I am afraid,
I put my trust in you.
In God, whose word I praise,
in God I trust; I shall not be afraid.
What can flesh do to me?

PSALM 56:3-4

Preaching to yourself is telling your soul what to do, even when you may not feel like it.

Write a note to yourself as David does in Psalm 56 (follow his pattern), and tell yourself how to address your fear.

I am sure that neither death nor life, nor angels nor rulers, nor things present nor things to come, nor powers, nor height nor depth, nor anything else in all creation, will be able to separate us from the love of God in Christ Jesus our Lord.

ROMANS 8:38-39

What causes you to feel distant from God's presence? Write your list below.

Read today's verse again and consider how nothing on your list can separate you from the love of Christ. Cross them out, one by one, and replace them with something that God has done to bring you near to Him.

Do not forsake wisdom, and she will protect you;
love her, and she will watch over you.
The beginning of wisdom is this: Get wisdom.
Though it cost all you have, get understanding.

PROVERBS 4:6-7 NIV

Ask the Lord for wisdom regarding a particular
circumstance in your life. Write it out, and be specific.

My goal is that they may be encouraged in heart and united in love,
so that they may have the full riches of complete understanding, in
order that they may know the mystery of God, namely, Christ, in
whom are hidden all the treasures of wisdom and knowledge.

COLOSSIANS 2:2-3 NIV

Can you remember a time when you could not make sense
of God's ways in your life, only to find understanding
and His good in them later? Recall and describe how
He was faithful in the mystery of His ways.

Surely he took up our pain
and bore our suffering,
yet we considered him punished by God,
stricken by him, and afflicted.
But he was pierced for our transgressions,
he was crushed for our iniquities;
the punishment that brought us peace was on him,
and by his wounds we are healed.

ISAIAH 53:4-5 NIV

What are the areas of pain in your life at the moment
—physically, emotionally, spiritually?

What are the words used to describe the
affliction Jesus endured on our behalf?

*Because all pain finds its origin in a fallen world, fallen
relationships, and our own fallen natures, consider how
the shed blood and broken body of Jesus makes peace
possible in each of the ways you currently feel pain.*

Write out a prayer of thanks in response to each area of pain and consider how Christ's suffering can cause you to rest right now.
(If you have trouble with this exercise,
read and think on Ephesians 2.)

Heal me, Lord, and I will be healed;
save me and I will be saved,
for you are the one I praise.

JEREMIAH 17:14 NIV

Pleading and praising often go hand in hand. Praise God for how
He has already saved and healed, and how He will again.

He [God] will wipe away every tear from their eyes, and death shall be no more, neither shall there be mourning, nor crying, nor pain anymore, for the former things have passed away.

REVELATION 21:4

If Jesus bore the greatest pain you would ever have to face, you can rest in knowing that He is at work, not only to redeem but also to restore. Revelation 21 provides a hope-filled picture of what that restoration will look like.

Offer back to the Lord those specific circumstances that you long to be "no more" and write them down here.

No more tears:

_____

_____

_____

_____

_____

_____

No more death:

_____

_____

_____

_____

_____

_____

No more sorrow:

_____

_____

_____

_____

_____

_____

No more pain:

_____

_____

_____

_____

_____

_____

No more regrets:

_____

_____

_____

_____

_____

_____

_____

About Benjamin he said:
"Let the beloved of the LORD rest secure in him,
for he shields him all day long,
and the one the LORD loves rests between his shoulders."

DEUTERONOMY 33:12 NIV

Our rest is so connected with our being securely loved. What
keeps you from resting in Him in your current season?

How does the truth that God's love for you is
secured in Christ affect the way you rest?

Return to your rest, my soul,
for the LORD has been good to you.

PSALM 116:7 NIV

Count your blessings one by one: How
has the Lord been good to you?

Yours, O Lord, is the greatness and the power and the glory and the victory and the majesty, for all that is in the heavens and in the earth is yours. Yours is the kingdom, O Lord, and you are exalted as head above all. Both riches and honor come from you, and you rule over all. In your hand are power and might, and in your hand it is to make great and to give strength to all.

1 CHRONICLES 29:11-12

Praising God for who He is and for His mighty works trains our hearts to rest in His character.

How has God's greatness, displayed on the earth and in all creation, caused you to trust Him?

In him we have obtained an inheritance, having been predestined according to the purpose of him who works all things according to the counsel of his will, so that we who were the first to hope in Christ might be to the praise of his glory.

EPHESIANS 1:11-12

Describe a time when God's ways in working "all things according to the counsel of his will" ultimately brought good in your life to the "praise of his glory."

Behold, the days are coming, declares the LORD, when I will make a new covenant with the house of Israel and the house of Judah, not like the covenant that I made with their fathers on the day when I took them by the hand to bring them out of the land of Egypt, my covenant that they broke, though I was their husband, declares the LORD. For this is the covenant that I will make with the house of Israel after those days, declares the LORD: I will put my law within them, and I will write it on their hearts. And I will be their God, and they shall be my people. And no longer shall each one teach his neighbor and each his brother, saying, "Know the LORD," for they shall all know me, from the least of them to the greatest, declares the LORD. For I will forgive their iniquity, and I will remember their sin no more.

JEREMIAH 31:31-34

What former place has the Lord brought you out of,
and how is He writing His promises on your heart anew?

I consider that the sufferings of this present time are not worth
comparing with the glory that is to be revealed to us.
For the creation waits with eager longing
for the revealing of the sons of God.

ROMANS 8:18-19

What changes are you eagerly longing to see...
in yourself, others, the world?

The Spirit himself testifies with our spirit
that we are God's children.
Now if we are children, then we are heirs—
heirs of God and co-heirs with Christ,
if indeed we share in his sufferings in order that
we may also share in his glory.

ROMANS 8:16-17 NIV

Describe what it means to be a child of God,
an heir to His kingdom, and a daughter of the King.

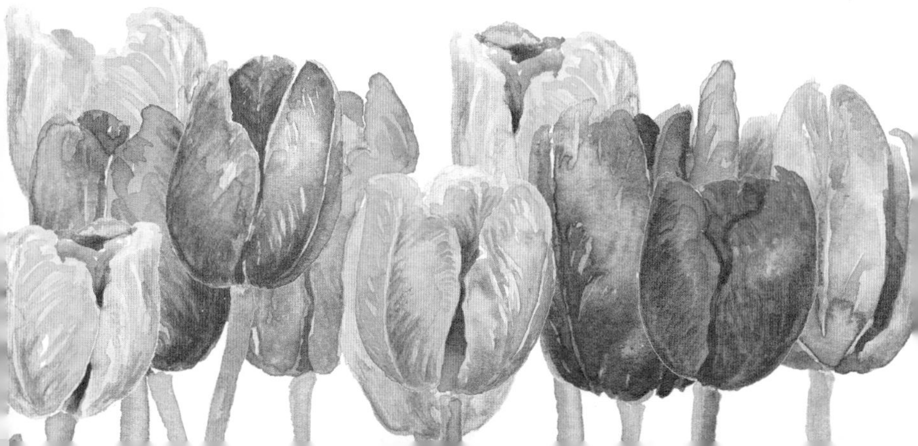

This is love: not that we loved God,
but that he loved us and sent his Son as an
atoning sacrifice for our sins.

1 JOHN 4:10 NIV

How has the Lord pursued you—found you
and redeemed you—with His love?

The Father himself loves you, because you have loved
me and have believed that I came from God.

JOHN 16:27

How is your relationship with your heavenly Father different
or similar to your relationship with your earthly father?

How does God's delight in you affect your identity?

See what kind of love the Father has given to us, that we should
be called children of God; and so we are. The reason why
the world does not know us is that it did not know him.

1 JOHN 3:1

How does believing that the Father delights in you,
His child, cause you to live differently?

Their minds were hardened. For to this day, when they read the old covenant, that same veil remains unlifted, because only through Christ is it taken away. Yes, to this day whenever Moses is read a veil lies over their hearts. But when one turns to the Lord, the veil is removed. Now the Lord is the Spirit, and where the Spirit of the Lord is, there is freedom.

2 CORINTHIANS 3:14-17

Only through Christ is the veil taken away.
Write a prayer of thanks for the freedom you have in Christ.

FREEDOM

Now before faith came, we were held captive under the law, imprisoned until the coming faith would be revealed. So then, the law was our guardian until Christ came, in order that we might be justified by faith. But now that faith has come, we are no longer under a guardian, for in Christ Jesus you are all sons of God, through faith. For as many of you as were baptized into Christ have put on Christ. There is neither Jew nor Greek, there is neither slave nor free, there is no male and female, for you are all one in Christ Jesus. And if you are Christ's, then you are Abraham's offspring, heirs according to promise.

GALATIANS 3:23-29

How did you come to faith in Jesus? Take your time and describe how you were once imprisoned in sin and hopelessness and are now released into freedom.

Know that the LORD, he is God!
It is he who made us, and we are his;
we are his people, and the sheep of his pasture.

PSALM 100:3

Begin a thorough list of all that God has made uniquely you.

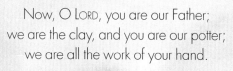

Now, O LORD, you are our Father;
we are the clay, and you are our potter;
we are all the work of your hand.

ISAIAH 64:8

Describe one way you've experienced God's shaping
and molding and forming you into His likeness.

Behold, blessed is the one whom God reproves;
therefore despise not the discipline of the Almighty.

JOB 5:17

In what ways have you experienced the Lord's
discipline, pruning, and reproof?

My son, do not despise the LORD's discipline
or be weary of his reproof,
for the LORD reproves him whom he loves,
as a father the son in whom he delights.

PROVERBS 3:11-12

Describe a time when the Lord's discipline resulted
in growth and unexpected beauty in your life.

The wisdom from above is first pure, then peaceable, gentle, open to reason, full of mercy and good fruits, impartial and sincere. And a harvest of righteousness is sown in peace by those who make peace.

JAMES 3:17-18

What would you say to your younger self about the wisdom of the Lord's pruning?

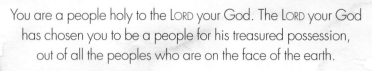

You are a people holy to the LORD your God. The LORD your God has chosen you to be a people for his treasured possession, out of all the peoples who are on the face of the earth.

DEUTERONOMY 7:6

What is your greatest possession,
and what would you do to protect what is yours?

MINE

Listen to me, O coastlands,
and give attention, you peoples from afar.
The LORD called me from the womb,
from the body of my mother he named my name.

ISAIAH 49:1

Your God knows you intimately; He's made you His own.
How does the truth that He calls you His
inform your identity today?

_____

_____

_____

_____

_____

_____

_____

_____

_____

_____

_____

_____

_____

_____

God is able to make all grace abound to you, so
that having all sufficiency in all things at all times,
you may abound in every good work.

2 CORINTHIANS 9:8

Describe a time when you felt deficient in your ability,
but God ultimately equipped you for what He called you to do.

He has saved us and called us to a holy life—not because of anything we have done but because of his own purpose and grace. This grace was given us in Christ Jesus before the beginning of time.

2 TIMOTHY 1:9 NIV

Write down and count the undeserved blessings God has placed in your life. Next to each blessing, describe how that blessing can be used for His purposes and to glorify Him with a holy life.

Now why do you wait?
Rise and be baptized and wash away your sins,
calling on his name.

ACTS 22:16

Are you waiting to come to the Lord with your needs?
What are the conditions you are waiting for, believing you
are not yet worthy or able to call upon your God?

Respond with a prayer, repenting from your self-imposed distance and alienation and confessing your need to come to Him.

Such is the confidence that we have through Christ toward God. Not that we are sufficient in ourselves to claim anything as coming from us, but our sufficiency is from God.

2 CORINTHIANS 3:4-5

What God-given, Christ-purchased qualifications make it possible for you to come into His presence?

My son, be attentive to my words;
incline your ear to my sayings.
Let them not escape from your sight;
keep them within your heart.
For they are life to those who find them,
and healing to all their flesh.
Keep your heart with all vigilance,
for from it flow the springs of life.

PROVERBS 4:20-23

If your life overflows from what feeds your heart, what are your heart and mind fixed upon today? What truths from God's Word must not escape your sight? Write them down (word for word from Scripture) and hide them in your heart.

ABOVE

Do not be conformed to this world,
but be transformed by the renewal of your mind,
that by testing you may discern what is the will of God,
what is good and acceptable and perfect.

ROMANS 12:2

What influences are shaping you?

What truths from God's Word
have impacted you recently?

We look not to the things that are seen
but to the things that are unseen.
For the things that are seen are transient,
but the things that are unseen are eternal.

2 CORINTHIANS 4:18

Write a letter to your younger self, telling her what
you've learned about the seen and unseen.

Do nothing from selfish ambition or conceit,
but in humility count others more significant than yourselves.

PHILIPPIANS 2:3

Pride is deceptive; it promises assurance and confidence
when it delivers only anxious self-preservation.
How have you seen the Lord calm your anxious
thoughts when you chose humility?

Who are the people you need to
humbly count as more important than yourself?

Humble yourselves before the Lord,
and he will lift you up.

JAMES 4:10 NIV

What prideful attitudes do you need to lay down?

Moses said to the people, "Fear not, stand firm, and see the salvation of the LORD, which he will work for you today. For the Egyptians whom you see today, you shall never see again. The LORD will fight for you, and you have only to be silent."

EXODUS 14:13-14

We have courage to stand fast when we know God is in command. He will fight for you—He already has, in the most significant way, through the cross!

Write about a time when you were able to stand firm in the face of fear and difficulty, knowing God was faithfully in control.

Only let your manner of life be worthy of the gospel of Christ, so that whether I come and see you or am absent, I may hear of you that you are standing firm in one spirit, with one mind striving side by side for the faith of the gospel.

PHILIPPIANS 1:27

Write a letter to someone who has encouraged you in steadfastness.

STAND

Let us hold fast the confession of
our hope without wavering,
for he who promised is faithful.

HEBREWS 10:23

Remind yourself of the hope that is immovable.
What promises from God's Word keep you standing firm?

But we have this treasure in jars of clay, to show that the surpassing power belongs to God and not to us. We are afflicted in every way, but not crushed; perplexed, but not driven to despair; persecuted, but not forsaken; struck down, but not destroyed; always carrying in the body the death of Jesus, so that the life of Jesus may also be manifested in our bodies. For we who live are always being given over to death for Jesus' sake, so that the life of Jesus also may be manifested in our mortal flesh. So death is at work in us, but life in you. Since we have the same spirit of faith according to what has been written, "I believed, and so I spoke," we also believe, and so we also speak, knowing that he who raised the Lord Jesus will raise us also with Jesus and bring us with you into his presence. For it is all for your sake, so that as grace extends to more and more people it may increase thanksgiving, to the glory of God. So we do not lose heart. Though our outer self is wasting away, our inner self is being renewed day by day. For this light momentary affliction is preparing for us an eternal weight of glory beyond all comparison.

2 CORINTHIANS 4:7-17

It is a hard truth that this body of ours is daily fading and will one day fail. What a glorious hope that our life in Christ is "being renewed day by day."

Take time to go back through this passage and recount the promises that Paul presents in these verses. Write them in your own words here.

Beloved, do not be surprised at the fiery trial when it comes upon you to test you, as though something strange were happening to you. But rejoice insofar as you share Christ's sufferings, that you may also rejoice and be glad when his glory is revealed.

1 PETER 4:12-13

How has suffering increased your faith and
revealed more of Christ in your life?

REJOICE

When you stand praying,
if you hold anything against anyone, forgive them,
so that your Father in heaven may forgive you your sins.

MARK 11:25 NIV

Any offense to you is a greater offense to the Father.
And yet He forgives. How much more can you?
What do you continue to hold against others?
Honestly write out your need to forgive these offenses.

Judge not, and you will not be judged; condemn not, and you will not be condemned; forgive, and you will be forgiven; give, and it will be given to you. Good measure, pressed down, shaken together, running over, will be put into your lap. For with the measure you use it will be measured back to you.

LUKE 6:37-38

Contrast a time that you have stood in judgment
with a time you have chosen to forgive.

If I then, your Lord and Teacher, have washed your feet, you also ought to wash one another's feet. For I have given you an example, that you also should do just as I have done to you. Truly, truly, I say to you, a servant is not greater than his master, nor is a messenger greater than the one who sent him.

JOHN 13:14-16

What is one way someone has washed your feet and served you?

Do nothing from selfish ambition or conceit, but in humility count others more significant than yourselves. Let each of you look not only to his own interests, but also to the interests of others. Have this mind among yourselves, which is yours in Christ Jesus, who, though he was in the form of God, did not count equality with God a thing to be grasped, but emptied himself, by taking the form of a servant, being born in the likeness of men. And being found in human form, he humbled himself by becoming obedient to the point of death, even death on a cross. Therefore God has highly exalted him and bestowed on him the name that is above every name, so that at the name of Jesus every knee should bow, in heaven and on earth and under the earth, and every tongue confess that Jesus Christ is Lord, to the glory of God the Father.

PHILIPPIANS 2:3-11

How is Jesus our example for meekness and humility?
In what ways does Jesus exemplify power under control?

Let no corrupting talk come out of your mouths,
but only such as is good for building up,
as fits the occasion, that it may
give grace to those who hear.

EPHESIANS 4:29

Are unwholesome talk and harsh words part of your communication
with others? Take time to confess this to the Lord and consider
how you need to build up people with your words.

Let us consider how to stir up one another to love and
good works, not neglecting to meet together, as is
the habit of some, but encouraging one another, and
all the more as you see the Day drawing near.

HEBREWS 10:24-25

Who has God put in your path to encourage?
How can you deliberately stir up their love and good deeds?

_____

_____

_____

_____

_____

_____

_____

_____

_____

_____

_____

_____

_____

_____

In his hand is the life of every living thing
and the breath of all mankind.

JOB 12:10

As the Sunday school song goes: "He's got the whole world
in His hands." What are you currently struggling to "hold
together" that really belongs in Jesus' capable hands?

I tell you, do not worry about your life, what you will eat or drink; or about your body, what you will wear. Is not life more than food, and the body more than clothes? Look at the birds of the air; they do not sow or reap or store away in barns, and yet your heavenly Father feeds them. Are you not much more valuable than they? Can any one of you by worrying add a single hour to your life? And why do you worry about clothes? See how the flowers of the field grow. They do not labor or spin. Yet I tell you that not even Solomon in all his splendor was dressed like one of these. If that is how God clothes the grass of the field, which is here today and tomorrow is thrown into the fire, will he not much more clothe you—you of little faith? So do not worry, saying, "What shall we eat?" or "What shall we drink?" or "What shall we wear?" For the pagans run after all these things, and your heavenly Father knows that you need them. But seek first his kingdom and his righteousness, and all these things will be given to you as well. Therefore do not worry about tomorrow, for tomorrow will worry about itself. Each day has enough trouble of its own.

MATTHEW 6:25-34 NIV

Make a list of all your needs, great and small, and then
compare your list to this familiar passage in Matthew.
How can you trust God's provision for your needs?

The Helper, the Holy Spirit, whom the Father will send
in my name, he will teach you all things and bring to
your remembrance all that I have said to you.

JOHN 14:26

God, the Holy Spirit, is our teacher.
Write a prayer to Him for understanding and wisdom.

May the God of hope fill you with
all joy and peace in believing,
so that by the power of the Holy Spirit
you may abound in hope.

ROMANS 15:13

Turn Paul's prayer into a personal prayer for yourself
and the people to whom you minister.

Cast your burden on the LORD,
and he will sustain you;
he will never permit
the righteous to be moved.

PSALM 55:22

Our burdens are not too heavy for Him to carry.
What are you shouldering today that was never
meant for you to bear on your own?

Praise be to the Lord, to God our Savior,
who daily bears our burdens.

PSALM 68:19 NIV

What makes Jesus strong enough, wise enough,
good enough, and trustworthy enough to bear our burdens?
Describe the Jesus you love and know,
who is capable of all this.

I will instruct you and teach you in the way you should go;
I will counsel you with my eye upon you.

PSALM 32:8

Are you looking for direction in a particular circumstance or
situation in your life? Where are you turning for counsel?

_____

_____

_____

_____

_____

_____

_____

_____

_____

_____

_____

_____

_____

_____

The light shines in the darkness,
and the darkness has not overcome it.

JOHN 1:5

How has the light of Jesus brought you out of darkness?

_____

_____

_____

_____

_____

_____

_____

_____

_____

_____

_____

_____

_____

_____

_____

_____

_____

_____

To us a child is born, to us a son is given;
and the government shall be upon his shoulder,
and his name shall be called
Wonderful Counselor, Mighty God,
Everlasting Father, Prince of Peace.

ISAIAH 9:6

Describe what peace looks like to you.

How has Jesus come to fulfill that hope for peace?

The peace of God, which surpasses all understanding, will guard your hearts and your minds in Christ Jesus.

PHILIPPIANS 4:7

Collect three truths from Scripture that stand guard over your heart and mind. Write them out and see how Jesus provides peace through each one.

PEACE

It is the LORD who goes before you.
He will be with you; he will not leave you or forsake you.
Do not fear or be dismayed.

DEUTERONOMY 31:8

Describe a time when God fulfilled His promise to
go before you. What circumstances are you going through
now in which you need to hold onto this promise?

The LORD will guide you continually
and satisfy your desire in scorched places
and make your bones strong;
and you shall be like a watered garden,
like a spring of water,
whose waters do not fail.

ISAIAH 58:11

List the provisions that the Lord has given to carry
you through difficult circumstances.

The LORD will fulfill his purpose for me;
your steadfast love, O LORD, endures forever.
Do not forsake the work of your hands.

PSALM 138:8

Pen a short prayer of thanks to the Lord
for how He's led you thus far, and how you see Him
fulfilling His purpose in you even now.

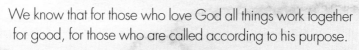

We know that for those who love God all things work together
for good, for those who are called according to his purpose.

ROMANS 8:28

What "all things" has God allowed
to work together for your good?
How have these things ushered you
further into your purpose to glorify God?

You are a chosen race, a royal priesthood, a holy nation, a people
for his own possession, that you may proclaim the excellencies
of him who called you out of darkness into his marvelous light.

1 PETER 2:9

Begin a list of how God has created you
on purpose and *for purpose.*

Be strong and courageous.
Do not fear or be in dread of them,
for it is the LORD your God who goes with you.
He will not leave you or forsake you.

DEUTERONOMY 31:6

Write a letter to your weary self and remind her of God's
faithfulness to follow through and complete His work in the
same way Moses encouraged the Israelites in Deuteronomy.

Let us not become weary in doing good,
for at the proper time we will
reap a harvest if we do not give up.

GALATIANS 6:9 NIV

Write a prayer of thanks to the Lord for promising to be the guarantor
of your faith, for sustaining you when you are weary, and for the
assurance He will complete what He has begun (Philippians 1:6).

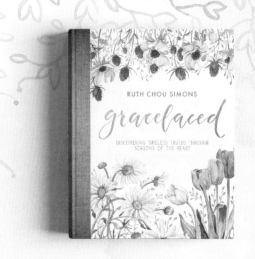

MORE BEAUTY AND TRUTH FROM
RUTH CHOU SIMONS...

Become immersed in carefully crafted meditations surrounded by hundreds of pieces of watercolor art in *Gracelaced: Discovering Timeless Truths Through Seasons of the Heart*. Featuring hand-lettered scriptures interwoven with the floral compositions Ruth Simons is known for, *Gracelaced* extends a soul-stirring invitation to draw close to God while...

- *resting* in who He is
- *rehearsing* the truth He says about you
- *responding* in faith to those truths
- *remembering* His provision to sustain you, time and time again

Who we are and *who God is* never changes, though everything else does. Let this book point you to truth as you journey through the changing seasons of your heart.

Ruth Chou Simons is an artist, writer, entrepreneur, and speaker. As the creator of the popular GraceLaced online shoppe, blog, and Instagram community, she shares scriptural truths daily through her hand-painted artwork and words. Ruth and her husband, Troy, live on the Western slope of Colorado and are grateful parents to six sons—their greatest adventure.